THE KNIGHT
A Jungian Healing Journey

Some Other Titles From New Falcon Publications

Aha! The Sevenfold Mystery of the Ineffable Love   –Aleister Crowley
Bio-Etheric Healing   –Trudy Lanitis
Undoing Yourself With Energized Meditation and Other Devices
Secrets of Western Tantra: The Sexuality of the Middle Path
Dogma Daze
   –Christopher S. Hyatt, Ph.D.
Rebels & Devils; The Psychology of Liberation
   –Edited by Christopher S. Hyatt, Ph.D.
Aleister Crowley's Illustrated Goetia
Taboo: Sex, Religion & Magick
Sex Magic, Tantra & Tarot: The Way of the Secret Lover
   –Christopher S. Hyatt, Ph.D., and Lon Milo DuQuette
Pacts With The Devil
Urban Voodoo: A Beginner's Guide to Afro-Caribbean Magic
   –Jason Black and Christopher S. Hyatt, Ph.D.
The Psychopath's Bible
   –Christopher S. Hyatt, Ph.D., and Jack Willis
Ask Baba Lon   –Lon Milo DuQuette
Aleister Crowley and the Treasure House of Images
   –J.F.C. Fuller, Aleister Crowley,
   Lon Milo DuQuette and Nancy Wasserman
Enochian World of Aleister Crowley
   –Lon Milo DuQuette and Aleister Crowley
Info-Psychology
Neuropolitique
The Game of Life
What Does WoMan Want?   –Timothy Leary, Ph.D.
Rebellion, Revolution and Religiousness   –Osho
Reichian Therapy: A Practical Guide for Home Use   –Dr. Jack Willis
Woman's Orgasm: A Guide to Sexual Satisfaction
   –Benjamin Graber, M.D., and Georgia Kline-Graber, R.N.
Shaping Formless Fire
Seizing Power
Taking Power   –Stephen Mace
The Illuminati Conspiracy: The Sapiens System –Donald Holmes, M.D.
An Insider's Guide to Robert Anton Wilson   –Eric Wagner
The Secret Inner Order Rituals of the Golden Dawn   –Pat Zalewski
Hinduism and Jungian Psychology
Sufism, Islam and Jungian Psychology   –J. Marvin Spiegelman, Ph.D.
Nonlocal Nature: The Eight Circuits of Consciousness
   –James A. Heffernan
on What is   –Ja Wallin

THE KNIGHT
A Jungian Healing Journey

SMALL GEMS BY

J. MARVIN SPIEGELMAN, Ph.D.

NEW FALCON PUBLICATIONS
Los Angeles, California, U.S.A.

Copyright © 1982 J. Marvin Spiegelman

All rights reserved. No part of this book,
in part or in whole, may be reproduced, transmitted,
or utilized, in any form or by any means, electronic or mechanical,
including photocopying, recording, or by any information storage
and retrieval system, without permission in writing
from the publisher, except for brief quotations
in critical articles, books and reviews.

ISBN 13: 978-1-56184-554-5
ISBN 10: 1-56184-554-5

First Edition 1982

New Falcon Publications Second Revised Edition 2021

The paper used in this publication meets the minimum requirements
of the American National Standard for Permanence of
Paper for Printed Library Materials Z39.48-1984

Printed in USA

NEW FALCON PUBLICATIONS

2046 Hillhurst Avenue
Los Angeles, CA 90027
www.newfalcon.com
email: info@newfalcon.com

CONTENTS

CHAPTER **1**
The Potentials of Active Imagination   1

CHAPTER **2**
Psycho-Mythology–A New Literary Genre   21

THE ADVENTURES OF THE KNIGHT

CHAPTER **3**
The King   33

CHAPTER **4**
The Old Woman   47

CHAPTER **5**
The Eye of God   57

CHAPTER **6**
The Snake   69

CHAPTER **7**
The Young Girl   79

CHAPTER **8**
The Tree of Life   95

CHAPTER 1
THE POTENTIALS OF ACTIVE IMAGINATION†

Active Imagination, Jung's technique of confrontation with the unconscious, is of central importance in his teaching yet is mentioned relatively little in his writings. His paper on *The Transcendental Function*, which singles out the topic for individual discussion, was written in 1916, but was not published until 1958, and then only at the behest of James Hillman who was looking for a contribution to the student publication of the C.G. Jung Institute, Zurich! Otherwise the topic is mentioned in the *Two Essays on Analytical Psychology, The Secret of the Garden Flower*, and with enormous significance attached to it, in his last great book, the *Mysterium Conjunctionis*. All of these are major works, it is true, but one would have thought that the tremendous importance of the topic, as shown most beautifully in his memoirs, *Memories, Dreams, Reflections*, would be repeatedly stressed at many opportunities. We shall have to ask ourselves the reason for this reticence but first it seems important to note that Jung's followers have also not been prolific on this topic. As to books, there is only Rix Weaver's *The Old Wise Woman*, and the privately printed monograph of Anna Marjula on *The Healing Influence of Active Imagination in a Specific Case of Neurosis**.

A handful of articles is all that I can find in a relatively cursory examination of the literature.

Babarah Hannah, in an enlightening and appreciative introduction to the book by Anna Marjula, quotes Jung as follows:

(Jung) regarded it (active imagination)–right to the end of his life–as our greatest help and support in establishing and keeping a balance between conscious and unconscious. He often regretted that it was not more widely used by his pupils and even once said to me: 'Active Imagination is the touchstone of whether anyone really wants to become independent through analysis or not.' When I asked him whether I might quote this remark, he replied: 'Not only may you, but I ask you to do so.'

The clarity of this quotation stands on its own, so when we ask why Jung does not mention the topic more often, we are more deeply than ever curious as to the answer. Before we come to this answer, however, we should perhaps define and elaborate what the method is all about. For this purpose, I have selected

---

***Barbara Hannah has included this monograph in a larger book on the topic**: *Active Imagination: Encounters with the Soul*, **Sigo Press, Santa Monica, CA 1981.**

Jung's description as given in his *Letters* (Vol I, pp. 458-460), in response to some questions written by a Mr. O in London, in April and May of 1947.

As you know, the principle of my technique does not consist only analysis and interpretation of such materials as are produced by the unconscious, but also in their synthesis by active imagination. (Jung goes to say this method is indicated do what we call in the German language the *"Auseinandersetzung mit dem Unbewussten"* **which is a dialectical procedure you carry through with yourself with the aid of active imagination. This is the best means I know to reduce the inordinate production of the unconscious...**

...The point is that you start with any image, for instance just with that yellow mass in your dream. Contemplate it and carefully observe how the picture begins to unfold or to change. Don't try to make it into something, just do nothing but observe what its spontaneous changes are. Any mental picture you contemplate in this way will sooner or later change through a spontaneous association that causes slight alteration of the picture. You must carefully avoid impatient jumping from one subject to another. Hold fast to the one image you have chosen and wait until it changes by itself. Note all these changes and eventually step into the picture yourself, and if it is a speaking figure and listen to what he or she has to say.

Thus you can not only analyse your unconscious but you also give your unconscious a change to analyse yourself, and therewith you gradually create the unity of conscious and unconscious without which there is no individuation at all.

It doesn't seem right that a man like yourself is still dependent upon analysts. It is also not good for you, because it produces again and again a most unwholesome dissociation of your opposites, namely pride and humility. It will be good for your humility if you can accept the gifts of the unconscious guide that dwells in yourself, and it is good for your pride to humiliate itself to such an extent that you can accept what you receive...

Did you never ask yourself what you receive... Did you never ask yourself who my analyst is? Yes, when it comes to the last issue, we must be able to stand alone *vis a vis* **the unconscious for better or worse.**

The last line, implying the capacity to "stand alone," is central and we shall return to this theme later on when we consider the underlying images or paradigms of the Jungian standpoint. Now, however, I wish to complete Jung's lively picture of the method by adding a summary of the important stages of the process, as outlined by Marie-Louise von Franz. I summarize the stages she mentions as follows:

1. To make one's consciousness empty; to stop the "mad mind," ego dialogue and chatter; to achieve

emptiness. This is done by many people now (e.g. in meditations of various kinds).

2. To allow emotions and fantasies to flow in.

3. To have it out with the unconscious: *auseinanderstzung*. The Jungian method is to confront; in the East one tends to ignore the fantasies. Confrontation is rather like the constant clinging to the changing Proteus in the myth.

A danger here is a "fictive ego," namely not having a true reaction (e.g. the lady who saw a lion at the seashore and merely looked. If it were a "true reaction," she would have jumped, fled, or something, not just looked). The attitude of the fictive ego results in a continuing split and nothing happens. A true reaction includes an ethical confrontation.

4. One then must draw conclusions in real life. Promises need to be kept when made with the figures of the unconscious and integrated into life.

Dr. von Franz points out that steps 3 and 4 are generally lacking in the psychological field.

Let us now return of the question as to why active imagination is so little mentioned. Jung, in his *Letters*, says that the method is hard to describe to "a merely intellectual public." Meier and Kirsch in the introduction to Weaver's book state that the method is "dangerous, needs a guru" to supervise. Barbarah Hannah, in the aforementioned introduction to Marjula's book, says that if done in the right way active imagination is "exceedingly hard work but not at all dangerous."

The danger, she goes on to point out, occurs if the method is done in the wrong way. This wrong way is any "fantasying out into the blue or indulging in fantasy, particularly in a wish-fulfilling way, or, perhaps even worse, uncritically living out emotions, such as hate and revenge, could even be described as pure poison."

Miss Hannah goes on to say that the key word is "active"–namely an active and hard work to restrain the rational mind, to observe and record correctly and to see when and how to intervene. She notes that people are usually just passive or only have "lousy excuses." Later on, we shall return to this issue when we consider the actual experience of active imagination with patients. One answer given to the objection that a guide is necessary is the book by Edwin Steinbrecher, *The Inner Guide Meditation*. Steinbrecher has been in Jungian analysis and tried active imagination while his analyst was away. He suddenly found himself paralyzed and in the grips of a devilish figure. He only gradually got himself out of it, but hit on his voyagings and questionings. This proved to be so easy and valuable that he devised a whole scheme whereby one may follow his method using his book alone, including such helps as tarot card images for specific archetypal figures and ways of using one's horoscope. He apparently has gotten good results with it. In effect, Steinbrecher agrees that a guru is necessary, but this guru, he says, is readily available within, if one just looks for it.

Steinbrecher's approach leads us to contrast Jung's active imagination with various kinds of procedures which might be called "guided fantasy." These latter methods are characterized by having a therapist or teacher provide specific images to be meditated upon, or directions to follow, rather than the attitude of Jung, which is to "let the soul speak for itself") Tertullian's famous statement). The methods of guided fantasy are carefully described and summarized in Mary Watkins recent work, *Waking Dreams*, in which she details the French, Italian and German work in these areas going back to Janet. For me it was enlightening to find that Janet, the teacher of Freud and Jung, actively engaged himself in the fantasies of his hysterical patients, trying to change outcomes and influence the unconscious directly. Jung was surely effected by this, but evolved his own method which markedly contrasts with the outwardly interventionist methods. But Jung also made a study of such "guided fantasy" methods, notably in his seminar on Loyola's *Exercitia Spiritualis* and various Eastern meditative methods.

I believe that one might say that Jung's method aims at widening of consciousness and the union of the latter with the unconscious, whereas the guided methods have a specific aim at effecting some kind of change. I have thought that one way of categorizing these divergent approaches was as the Magical and the Mystical. The magical methods aim at power, at effect, and control. The mystical methods, in contrast, aim at love, at relationship, and surrender. Some of the Eastern methods, looking toward union and surrender, can also be characterized as mystical, as can Jung's. But Jung's method is unique in "letting the soul speak for itself" and specifically working toward the integration of conscious and unconscious.

It might be well to conclude this overview of active imagination with a summary of the values to be found for those who undertake the method: (1) one becomes less dependent upon an analyst; ultimately one becomes one's own analyst; (2) one is less dependent upon dreams for finding out what the unconscious is intending; (3) there is a widening of consciousness; (4) pursued to the end, one ultimately finds all the things that Jung discovered and wrote about: shadow, anima/animus, old wise man and woman, mana personality, and Self. In short, it is the ideal experimental method to ascertain for one's self what Jung experienced; (5) the method can lead to wholeness, integration of the personality, the transcendent function; (6) to quote Jung at the very end of his paper on the *Transcendent Function*: "It is a way of attaining liberation by one's own efforts and finding the courage to be one's self."

ACTIVE IMAGINATION IN THE THERAPEUTIC PRACTICE

With such an important, powerful and valuable addendum to therapeutic practice in the armamentarium of the Jungian analyst, one would think that the method would be widely used. Alas, this is not the case. Relatively few patients do it at all, and of those that do, few go more than part way with it. And even fewer see the method through to the relativization of the ego, the relation of ego to the larger totality of the self, and produce the kind of mandala symbolism so fully described by Jung in his various publications.

What are the reasons for this? One might say that the method is not culturally supported, particularly in such an extraverted country as the United States. But Miss Hannah also reports that even in her practice in Zurich, the center of analytic psychology and of introversion as a national and local viewpoint, the method is not widely used. Therefore, the answer of lack of cultural support is not enough. Other reasons that emerge are that patients have other concerns, such as adaptation to the world, problems of love, occupation, relationship, which are not the same as reconciling conscious with unconscious. Furthermore, it is said that patients are not "up to it," are not in the "second half of life" struggles. Or, one can follow Jung's and Hannah's comment that patients–and analysts–just have "lousy excuses."

The problem of "lousy excuses"–and the reason for this lying in the fact that active imagination is "hard work"–can be overcome by being rather less classical in one's demand or expectation that the procedure needs to be done by the patient alone, in his/her own room. If one permits or asks for fantasies in the course of the session, and follows the central

Jungian viewpoint of focusing upon the images, then the same material and transformations do occur. The results, of course, is less "pure" and one is not close to combinations of "guided fantasy" with "letting the soul speak for itself," but it is notable that even Mrs. Jung suggested that the patient should apply directly to "some positive female archetype, such as the Great Mother." Such combinations are now, indeed, part of the work of other schools of therapy, such as Gestalt therapy and Psychosynthesis. These patients who come to Jungian work from such other schools often fin a useful deepening of understanding provided by archetypal theory. Conversely, it seems to me that this use of fantasy within the analytic hour and consequent immersion of the process within the therapeutic relationship does facilitate its use and vitiates the problem of "lousy excuses."

A superiority is sometimes assumed by those who do active imagination ("really Jungian") in contrast to those who do not ("really Freudian" or "involved in the transference"). Fordham, for example, emphasizes the transference and avers that one needs "maturity" to do active imagination, which can happen only after there is healing, through the transference, and enhancement of the capacity to be alone and to fantasy. Jung, on the other hand, says that the transference itself leads to active imagination, since the needs, expectations and projections can only be resolved that way.

In my view, these are really two different ways of taking on the unconscious. Active imagination relates to the unconscious in a *vertical* dimension, whereas transference, and by extension, working with relationship, is taking on the unconscious in the *horizontal* dimension. The former leads to the experience of the "God–Within," as I have called it, whereas the latter leads to the "God–Among." (See below on Mutual process and joint active imagination.) One can see that the relationship to one's self (active imagination) is naturally complemented by a psychological relationship with another person and *vice-versa*.

A further limitation of active imagination, even when pursued to the "end," is that the method does not seem to effect, positively, one's relation to the "world," except by the withdrawal of projections. An exception, of course, is that method regularly leads to the occurrence of synchronistic events, in which one is related to the world in a deep, mystical way. The ongoing, *reciprocal* relationship with outer reality, however, remains essentially untouched. The hope, of course, is that one is so changed by inner work that the "world" also changes–at least one's relationship to it. This image, fantasy, or expectation is a central one in Jungian psychology and might be called "The Rainmaker Image." It is based on the following story, told by the Sinologist, Richard Wilhelm:

Richard Wilhelm was in a remote Chinese village which was suffering from a most unusually prolonged drought. Everything had been done to put an end to it, and every kind of prayer and charm had been used, but all to no avail. So the elders of the village told Wilhelm that the only thing to do now was to send for a rainmaker from a distance. This interested him enormously and he was careful to be present when the rainmaker arrived. He came in a covered car, a small wizened old man. He got out of the car, sniffed the air in distaste, then asked for a cottage on the outskirts of the village. He made the condition that no one should disturb him and that his food should be put down outside the door. Nothing was heard of him for three days, then everyone woke up to a downpour of rain. It even snowed, which was unknown at that time of year.

Wilhelm was greatly impressed and sough out the rainmaker, who had now come out of his seclusion. Wilhelm asked him in wonder: "So you can make rain?" The old man scoffed at the very idea and said "of course" he could not. "But there was the most persistent drought until you came," Wilhelm retorted, " and then–within three days– it rains?" "Oh," replied the old man, "that was something quite different. You see, I come from a region where everything is in order, it rains when it should and is fine when that is needed, and the people also are in order and in themselves. But

that was not the case with the people here, they were all out of Tao and out of themselves. It was at once infected when I arrived, so I had to be quite alone until I was once more in Tao and then naturally it rained!"

This "Rainmaker Image," I believe, is a central one in Jung's psychology. The valuing of Man Alone is surely the archetypal foundation toward which active imagination aims and from which it has its origins. Insofar as the Rainmaker is effective, one can be glad. Alas, this is not always the case, and the world sometimes requires other method of effecting it. One can say, then, that the limits of active imagination are also those of the Rainmaker.

Another limitation of active imagination is that there is rarely enough concreteness or body to it. The favorite methods are auditory, visual and in writing, which are particularly easy for the intuitive introvert, but can readily leave out the fourth function of sensation, as I personally can painfully attest. Even when drawing, painting and even sculpture and dance are included in the work, one increasingly includes sensation and body, but only partly, in my opinion. This has become apparent to me from Reichian therapy, which approaches the rigidities of "muscular armoring" as it exists in the body. Even dancers and athletes, for example, are often among the most "armored" of people. Active imagination can be enhanced, I think, with other meditative methods and body work (see below).

One might say that active imagination accomplishes very well the alchemical phase of the *unio mentalis*, but the *conjunctio* (union with the body) and the *unus mundus* (union with the world, and the experience of world unity) occurs only partly or temporarily in my opinion.

Finally, along the dimension of Personal and Impersonal, the method can lead to a predominance of the impersonal. As a result of the work, there often occurs a kind of detachment which fits in well with the Rainmaker image of relation to life. This is seen as positive, in the Eastern sense, but sometimes one encounters individuals who are somewhat aloof and impervious as a result of the method, and not infrequently, of the type mentioned sadly by Guggenbuhl as lacking in eros, impenetrable, and rigid. "Body" and "World" the, as well as "Eros" are the complements to this limitation. Ultimately, of course, our aim is to combine the personal and impersonal, else our wholeness is mere sham.

BOUNDARIES AND POSSIBILITIES FOR DEVELOPMENT

My personal work with active imagination began shortly after I started analysis at the age of twenty-four, and this constituted a more-or-less regular activity, in analysis and outside of it, for sixteen years. At the end of the year in 1966, I was engaged in a long-term fantasy of being in a cave with a Mother and Daughter, as Wise Old Man, and a child who did not speak when suddenly a Knight appeared and carried off the Mother and Daughter. Surprised, I recognized the Knight as a figure from a dream earlier in the year who said to me that "we no longer had a cause to serve," referring to the Jungian collective as such (I had occasion to resign from my local analytic society earlier in the year). Now, this Knight said, he was trying to get my attention and that he had some tales to tell which might be useful for me and others also. There were several in his realm who wished to tell their stories, too. I was not to be a mere amanuensis, the task requiring my full participation. Would I be willing? I replied that I had a busy practice, teaching, a family and social life, but I could provide two days a week for that purpose if that were enough. The Knight agreed, and then began a series of tales which involved me deeply for a number of years.

The first story of the Knight, a kind of gnostic adventure, was followed by a love story of an Arab, and a tale of a Japanese Ronin, using the Zen Ox-Herding pictures as a base. Thereafter came tales of Julia, the Atheist-Communist, Sybilla the Nymphomaniac, and Maria the Nun. Following them were an alchemical tale of The African, a Kundalini adventure by May the Yogini, the Old Chinese Man who dialogued with the I Ching, and finally a Kabbalistic endeavor to under stand the Holocaust by Sophie-Sarah the Medium. A series of psalms by each of them concluded the book. These people each had an individuation story to tell, all meeting at the Tree of Life in paradise. The resultant book, *The Tree: A Jungian Journey–Tales in Psycho-Mythology*, (Falcon Press, 1982, first issued 1975)); constituted a new genre, in my view, a kind of science-fiction, in which psychological knowledge is combined in fiction to produce "psycho-mythology." The following book in the series is *The Quest: Further Adventures in the Unconscious*, New Falcon Publications.

This extension of active imagination raised several questions. The first problem is to distinguish between active imagination as a form of personal growth and the products thereof as a kind of art. In his memoirs, Jung speaks of being tempted to view his material as art, but he kept his scientific and psychological orientation. In his view, the work needed both understanding and an aesthetic attitude, but if one thought the product was art, there was danger of losing its proper aim. That is certainly possible, but I think that one can now allow a little more leeway to the artistic side, since Jung has established the method quite firmly. For it to be considered art, he work must clearly be at a transpersonal level.

Secondly, a question arises as to how to consider the ego in such works of psycho-mythology. My own experience was to relate to these figures as they would address me, but to be loosely identified with them when they were undergoing their own experience. I see this as a connection with a "transcendental ego," as it were, rather as if, in Kabbalistic terms, I would move from my ordinary ego in Malkuth (body, flesh region), to unite with the archetypal figure (e.g. knight) of hero or heroine at the level of Tiphareth (God-Man condition), enabling us to then relate to the God/-Gods at the higher levels. This allows, or helps to produce, a more flexible and multi-faceted ego, which can, in turn, face and serve more multitudinous aspects of the Self.

Another extension of active imagination came for me not only in my work alone, but as a consequence of the experience of the transference in analytical work. I had found, fairly early on, that the implications of the transference were such that the archetypes were affecting both therapist and patient and, with many, the work gradually became a mutual one, in which both parties were transformed. We are then dealing with the "God–Among" as well as the traditional "God–Within." I called this Mutual Process. In this process, the participants can sometimes work with fantasy, particularly images of each other, as wrapped in archetype and projection. This becomes a form of Joint Active Imagination. With one person, for example, after the regular analytic work was completed, we met regularly for some two years, working on joint paintings. But joint active imagination can be a regular part of the work in almost any analytic process, particularly when the transference is at issue. From this point of view, the underlying model of the work, in contrast to the "Rainmaker" model, is alchemical, that of the alchemical and his *soror mystica*, as Jung describes in his *Psychology of the Transference*.

A different extension of Joint Active Imagination has been undertaken by my colleague, Lawrence Kovalenko, and her associate, Dooley Brown, who have for some time been pursuing a kind of psychomythology together, producing a work which extends into new dimensions. Their work, not yet published, is both fictional and scientific, bringing forward some discoveries about the unconscious which are rather startling and are subject to scientific test.

Earlier, I suggested that active imagination was probably deficient in the connection with and transformation of body energies and matter. Interestingly, the working with given images, matter and "energies" is the traditional domain of magic. The foremost living authority in magic has written an important treatise in which he tries to combine the principles of magic (including the meditation upon and working with "energies" in an imaginative method) with the principles of analytical psychology, a book curiously unknown in Jungian circles: Israel Regardie, *The Middle Pillar, a Co-Relation of the Principles of Analytical Psychology and the Elementary Techniques of Magic*. The problems of combining psychology, particularly Jungian psychology, with Magic and other occult work are discussed in my paper, *Psychology and the Occult*."

Another circle is completed when we consider the advanced work in bio-feedback, a use of fantasy which seems quite magical, and is aimed at effecting both nervous systems by means of meditative or imaginative processes. Thus, it seems to me, the imaginative processes. Thus, it seems to me, the imaginative method of Jung extends itself into realms of spirit and matter, fully consonant with the experience of the archetypes and is a fitting sequel to his work.

In concluding let me sum up:

A. Active imagination is the method *par excellence* for coming to terms with the unconscious and in finding one's own wholeness or Self.

B. It is largely effective in the soul/spirit dimension and in aspects of introversion, but less so in the extraverting aspects of relationship, connection with the world, and, in the other direction, with body energies, physiology, and matter.

C. Extensions of the method into "psycho-mythology" and "join active imagination" are promising, as well as the related developments in the area of guided fantasy, magic, and biofeedback.

† **The chapter on** *Potentials of Active Imagination,* **was given as a lecture to the Analytical Psychology Club of London at the Royal Society of Medicine on March 15, 1979.**

A revised version was published in *Harvest: Journal for Jungian Studies,* **London, November 1981.**

CHAPTER 2
PSYCHO-MYTHOLOGY

"Active fantasy being the principle attributes of the artistic mentality, the artist is not merely representer, he is also a creator, hence essentially an educator since his works have the value of symbols that trace out the line of future development. Whether the actual social validity of the symbol is more general or more restricted depends upon the quality or vital capacity of the creative individuality."*

With the term, "psycho-mythology," I wish to introduce a new literary genre which bears a familial resemblance to both science-fiction and the historical novel. In these forms, there is a peculiar kind of union of the opposites of fact and fiction. Science-fiction starts with current scientific knowledge, makes reasonable extrapolations toward future discoveries, and fuses these with fantasy. Historical novels add romance, conjectured conversation and embellishment to what is known of recorded events. In both cases, the structure of "truth" and "reality" is enriched by imagination, which is psychological truth.

* C. G. Jung, *Psychological Types* (1, p.580 f)

"Psycho-methodology" stands for a similar union of fact and imagination, but in this field there is a marriage of psychological knowledge with the type of fantasy that reaches the universal, archetypal, mythological level. I am not referring to the well-known psychological novel, which uses the insights of psychology to probe the depths of a particular personality. That form is closer to the genre of the detective story or the clinical case study, although it can reach heights of artistic excellence as, for example, in Dostoevsky's *Crime and Punishment*.

Rather than concerning itself with the motivations of an individual, psycho-mythology relates to the collective psyche and its' drama. Paradoxically, the perturbations of the modern man, occupied with his struggle for individuation, is both the source and core of it. The reason for this is that the invention of discovery of this genre came out of sixteen years of experience of C.G. Jung's "Active Imagination) (2).

Psycho-mythology is a literature in which an individual's fantasy transcends the personal level, reaching the collective unconscious. In addition, the work is consciously connected with either available religious or mythical material and is clearly intended as a work of art. With this definition, the genre is seen to straddle both what has been customarily called Active Imagination, as taught by Jung, and Art. In active imagination, the intention is a confrontation by the individual with the unconscious, with the aim of expanding his consciousness and fostering individuation and wholeness. In art, the intention is to produce an esthetically satisfying work, which may communicate some quality or experience to others, or may be for itself alone. In art, any development of consciousness or wholeness in the artist is largely incidental. Indeed, there are those who claim that the intrusion of psychological need for growth of consciousness, with the artistic need of esthetics, communication, and for its' own sake.

Before I relate how I came to discover or create this genre, I would like to say a few more words about Jung and active imagination. As is well-known to all who have read Jung's wonderful and remarkable autobiography, *Memories, Dreams and Reflections* (3), the great psychologist discovered the method of confrontation with the unconscious after he had broken with Freud. At that time, he was isolated, did not know his direction, and was convinced that he had no personal myth at all. He began to play with his fantasy and with the figures who emerged in that plat and from his dreams. He was the first to take the products of that play seriously and to relate to the dwellers of the unconscious as if they were as real as any Swiss Burgher that one might meet strolling the Limat in Zurich. He realized that these figures, though autonomous, were products of his own soul and he undertook a relationship with them.

In this process, Jung changed both the unconscious and himself. Greatly moved by this activity, which lasted several years in his late thirties, he made most of the discoveries which were to be developed during the remainder of his life. The importance of Active Imagination, therefore, was as central for Jung as was the focus upon dreams. Yet he was reluctant to publish very much on this topic. He did produce some work in this area (1, 2) and others are now following upon this beginning (6).

Jung's reluctance in publishing on the topic of Active Imagination was strange since he thought this method would ultimately free an individual from dependence upon any analyst at all! He says this beautifully in his Letters (4, pp. 458-461). He recognized that the work of Active Imagination contained both the need for Understanding (which was the effort to raise consciousness) and the Aesthetic (for beautiful and satisfying expression). In his earliest work on the topic (2), he clearly perceived that the method would lead now one way and now the other, yet he was adamant in asserting that this material was surely not art, but had a psychological aim.

The reason for Jung's assertion, in my opinion, comes from his experience of the female personage (whether a fantasy "anima' person or a concrete, living one) mentioned in his autobiography (3). That lady, when shown the beautiful paintings and writings of the artist-poet that Jung was, said that he should be and was an artist. Jung hotly denied this, saying that he was a scientist! I think that Jung, struggling to keep his psychological discoveries in the realm of science, had to lean over backwards and even sacrifice the true artistic value of some of what he produced. Those who have seen some of the paintings of the Red Book in the film of Jung, or read the poetry of his "Sermons of the Dead" (5), already know his artistic capacity. Furthermore, those of us who follow Jung appreciate the scientific value of his discoveries, no longer need to keep the method of Active Imagination strictly in the psychological worker-basket, and can allow its' expansion in other ways.

Another hindrance to Active Imagination becoming better known lies not with Jung alone, but also with some of his followers. There are those who are fearful of speaking about it, believing it to be a tool of the second half of life alone, and a dangerous one at that, properly limited to those who are supervised in analysis (6). I am less fearful, having discovered that the technique is difficult for most people to embark upon, quite demanding of discipline and commitment to stay with, thus outside the grasp of the merely dilettante. As for possible danger, the psyche seems to have its' natural protections of boredom, fear, skepticism, or inflation, all of which dissuade the non-devoted. I would add that from the artistic standpoint, probably even fewer of those who embark upon this work will produce material which, as Jung has said, will "communicate with the past and with the future, as well as with contemporaries" (1, pp. 574 f).

A further consideration of Active Imagination can be found in the references. At this point, I wish to tell the story of how I happened upon psycho-mythology." But, before I do, I feel the necessity of mentioning other available examples of the field. Strictly speaking, there are none, since the method has grown out of Jung's discoveries and his psychology, so that only the future will produce such works of art. Yet there are forerunners, I think, such as Goethe's *Faust*, or Thomas Mann's *Holy Sinner*, to mention only very great ones. These works, one can see, meet the definition of carrying religious-mythological significance, are psychologically insightful, reach the collective psyche, as well as intending artistic expression. They also carry both individual and collective significance simultaneously. Perhaps you can think of other examples.

Now to the story of my stories. On December 28, 1966, I was seated at my desk in my office, reflecting upon the preceding year's events, which had been painful, momentous and shattering for me. During that year, I had found it necessary to resign from my local professional analytic society and to break off some relationships which had proved to be illusory. That day, I was engaged in active imagination, which had been my custom at least twice a week for many years. I had started this process just a few months after beginning my own analysis in 1950 and had continued with it, with only a two year interruption during military service, ever since. It had proved to be especially valuable when I ceased working with any analyst at all some three years previous.

The particularly fantasy I had been working on for some months involved being in a cave with an old man, a woman and her daughter, and a young boy with dark eyes who did not speak. I was talking withe group when suddenly a huge Knight, wearing black armor with a golden sun emblazoned on his breast-plate, broke in, abducted the mother and daughter, riding away on his horse. I recognized this Knight from a dream I had had some six months earlier. In that dream, which took place after I resigned from the professional society, this Knight appeared and said to me that the had been at my side for a long time, but that now we no longer had a cause to serve. I understood him to mean the collective Jungian cause, as it worked as an institution in the world. I was aware, also, that the Knight was representative of my own inner "hero" figure, going back to early childhood. At the age of three, for example, I had a powerful experience of sitting on my tricycle and feeling the power of God high above and warming me from the sun, and also located inwardly, as an equal power, at my chest.

Now this dream hero appeared in earnest and was carrying off two important feminine figures. I pursued him, continuing my fantasy, and asked him why he did that and what he wanted. The Knight replied that he abducted those ladies in order to get my full attention and that he had some stories to tell. Would I be interested in hearing them, he wondered? He also hinted that there were other people there who had tales to tell, should I be inclined to take the time to hear them and work with them. He suggested that these stories were important for others to hear, as well as for myself. Excitedly, but somewhat skeptically, I agreed to attend to these tales, provided the work could be kept within the periods I have available for such activity. After all, I had patients, family, and other demands upon my time. He agreed, and then began the work which was to take most of two days a week for several years. The Knight's tale was followed by that of a Moslem Arab, a Japanese Buddhist Ronin, and then by three women: Julia, the Atheist-Communist, Sybilla, the Nymphomaniac, and Maria, the Nun. Thereafter came stories by the African, which was alchemical in nature, Maya, the Yogini who performed a kind of Kundalini Yoga, the tale of the Old Chinese Man who struggled with the spirit of the *I Ching*, and finally, the Medium, a woman named Sophie-Sarah who embraced Kabbalah.

These ten people each told a story of their own individuation, and each represented a different religion or syncretism, or some meditative, consciousness-seeking activity. Each was rather unorthodox, yet all found themselves at the Tree of Life. Altogether, their tales constituted what came to be called *The Tree*.

This series, some six hundred typewritten pages in length, was barely completed when there appeared another person, who called himself the Son of the Knight. This chap pursued a different series of myths, and this second book took up his quest, and also that of a Mother and Daughter in a cave, a part of the Grail legend involving King Arthur, Lancelot, and Queen Guinevere. That four-hundred page book was called, *The Quest*.

I must add that I was no mere amanuensis to these story-tellers. I often found myself not only relating their tales, but also living them and identifying with them as each of them approached the Gods. I worked and learned with them, although my true ego place seems to be somewhere else, more like the present narrator, but also as multiple and various as all of these, my deep inner friends. It remains for our mutual work to go out to the world and walk among men. "Let each know where the other is," was the message to the Knight, and so say I, too.

THE ADVENTURES
OF THE KNIGHT

CHAPTER 3
THE KING

Once there was a vicious King who lived in a hollow shell in the bottom of the Sea. He was hidden from sight, but because of his evil emanations, he was able to create havoc in the world just by means of his dark thoughts and ill feelings. He had been there for centuries, causing great pain to people, but since no one knew where to find him, they could not understand the cause of their misery and blamed their suffering on "the times", the weather, their leaders, and, of course, their neighbors.

At the time my story begins, I was a young Knight, naive and foolhardy. I had already had adventures aplenty, more with women, perhaps, than battles with other Knights, and I was far from serious. Pleasure was my aim.

One day, however, as I was walking peacefully in the forest, leading my horse to drink at a stream, there appeared before me an Angel of God. It was an astounding thing, and shocking, but just as real as this moment. The Angel was not loving and gentle with me. He was stern and firm.

"Knight," he said, "you have sought after adventure and pleasure. That is all right for a young man, but something more must be made of your life now. It has been decreed that you be sent to the vicious King at the bottom of the Sea, and that you reform him or kill him, as you see fit. There is to be no reward for this. Your only recompense is that you do something more with your life than you have thus far." With that the Angel vanished. He did not ask me if I agreed to take on this task. Nor did he direct me as to how I was to proceed.

I sat down by the stream and stroked the flanks of my horse, wondering at what had happened. I knew that I was no saint, but I did not think that I was so different from other knights as to merit either the particular censure or the special task. As I sat there musing about this event, I noticed that my horse pricked up his ears and started to tremble. I had not noticed how he had reacted to the appearance of the Angel, but now he seemed to know something that I did not. He pranced about impatiently, as if eager to be off. Thinking that perhaps the Angel was sending his messages through my horse to me, I got on my horse's back, let the reins hang loose, and allowed him to go where he would.

At once, he bounded off in a northerly direction, as if he knew exactly where he was going. We rode all day, stopping only for water. Towards evening, we came to the Sea–I know not which–and there the horse halted. I dismounted, tired and wet with perspiration. I sat quietly, apprehensive at what might happen to me. This was no ordinary adventure I knew, and I was no more accustomed to being guided by my horse than I was to the appearance of angels. I looked at my charger and was surprised to see him calm and hardly tired. He grazed peacefully, just as if this were an ordinary day.

I sat and waited. I watched my horse to see if other guidance would be forthcoming, but he behaved just as he had that morning, before the Angel appeared. I looked out over the Sea and saw nothing. Soon it grew dark and cold. I wrapped my blanket around me, with the thought that if the Angel had some desire of me, he would come in his own time and not at my behest. I made a fire and ate what little food I had left. Soon I was lost in dreams–not of adventure, but of a joyous and peaceful life in a pleasant castle with lovely maidens and friends. While enjoying this fantasy, however, I again saw the stern face of the Angel, appearing now in a cloud. He simply shook his head back and forth, as if to say, as he had done that morning, that this life of pleasure and ease was not to be for me. Again, no direction, only a firm "No."

I awakened in the morning, refreshed, though dampened in spirit. I found some fruit and ate thoughtfully. I waited for a sign, but nothing happened. I waited in the heat of the day and the silence of the afternoon. No sign. I was beginning to feel the fool. What a silly fellow I had been, thought I, to let a vision lead me and to put myself under the guidance of a horse! I wondered if it would not be best to quietly retrace my steps and never tell anyone about this peculiar experience. But something made me stay on. Again night fell, and again nothing happened. And so it was the next day and the next. Not until seven days had elapsed, by which time I was tired, irritated, disgruntled, and hungry, did the Angel appear again.

This time, just at sunset, he came walking out of the water and stopped some twenty paces from me. He spoke in a clear, cool voice, not quite as stern as before, but still unloving. "Knight," he said, "you have waited as instructed." (Instructed, thought I, by whom? I waited because I did not know what else to do.) "You are willful and arrogant and I do not know why you have been chosen for this task. But it is not in my province to choose, only to convey. Tomorrow morning you will walk out into the water with your horse. You must trust him to lead you in your task." Thus speaking, the Angel disappeared. I must admit that it was a relief to finally have some indication that my first vision wasn't the last. If this were an aberration, at least it was consistent. I minded madness less than being a fool in those days.

The next morning I awakened early, and made ready to do as the Angel commanded. I mounted my charger and rode into the Sea. It was not so easy, since the waves pushed us back. We clung to the floor of the Sea, however, and I fought against my natural impulse to swim. Following instructions, I gripped the mane and neck of my horse and held my breath as long as I could. I felt my lungs would collapse, was about to gasp for air and drown in water when I lost consciousness.

Some time passed, I know not how long. When I awakened, I was at the bottom of the Sea, inside a hollow shell. I found that I could breath naturally. With me was my horse. The shell was about as large as an ordinary room and had a faint glow in it–a blue light from an unknown source. The shell was barren, like a monk's cell or a cave, but a few paces away was the figure of a man. He was old and bearded. He wore a crown. Here, I thought, was the vicious King that I was sent to reform or kill.

The King looked at me kindly. He waited until I had fully recovered my senses, then spoke to me. His voice was gentle, yet strong.

"I suppose, Knight," he said, "you have been sent here either to kill me or reform me." I was astonished at this and wondered if this creature were so wily as to know all that transpired out on the land. I reflected that since he could cause so much harm, he must, indeed, know a great deal. I felt that I must be wary of him, but kindness, warmth, and strength disarmed me. Since he knew so much anyway, I conclude, I decided to be open and honest with him. I therefore nodded my head "Yes" in answer to his remark. He sighed at this and seemed to vanish inside himself, lost with his thoughts. I waited respectfully, saying nothing, and soon he began to speak, slowly and sadly.

"It has been so for centuries. Young, brave knights are sent to kill me or reform me. I seek not war, nor violence. I seek only to live in peace. I was once a great King in the world, governed as best I could, and, I think, led a happy kingdom. We tried to live in justice and love. We cared for one another. Each person struggled to develop his own soul, and worked toward the mutuality of being brothers and sisters. Our land flourished. We had pain and sadness, as well as joy, but somehow we grew in understanding and in love. But then it happened that a lasting sadness came over our land. There was bickering and anger. There was dastardly and greed. There was hatred. Of course, we had always had these things, which were painful to us, but now they exceeded our endurance. Worst of all, there was great injustice of each toward each. We could not understand it. We asked our wise men and our wise women, but none could explain.

"Finally, an Angel if the Lord appeared. He appeared before all of us so that all could see, and he spoke sternly. He said that the ravages of the land were all to be laid at my door. He said that I was ambitious and full of pride. He said, even, that I wanted to be God. The people and I were shocked at these accusations and I shook my head in disbelief. The Angel said that the only thing that would remedy the situation would be for me to sacrifice my son, and for me to be banished into a nether world where I would no longer cause havoc to the people. Now, I did not mind being banished, since I was, by nature, a rather retiring man, and I was certainly prepared to give up my rulership if it was the source of such grief and destruction to the people. But my son I loved dearly. He seemed wiser and more full of joy than myself. He seemed to be the natural heir to what I had achieved and would fulfill our hopes more than any of us could. To sacrifice him seemed sore and painful. There seemed no way out, however. The Angel was stern and implacable.

"My son was taken from me and crucified and I have been banished here, at the bottom of the Sea.

I can neither die nor live, but remain here, alone with my thoughts and my speculations. The sorrow of my son's sacrifice had diminished with the years–it is many centuries now. But I am not allowed to remain in peace. Every century or so, a Knight like yourself is sent to reform me or kill me. It seems as if the world continues in its grief and agony and inequality, and blame for this is laid at my doorstep. For I, it seems, am the vicious King who is the cause of the darkness. I do not understand it. I have no ill will, desire no power, and certainly do not wish to cause the people trouble, but I am thought to be the Devil, it seems. I am neither God nor Devil, but simply a human King who has been allowed to neither live nor die. Many are the Knights who have been sent to kill me or reform me. They have been of all nations and creeds and temperaments. I have been very willing to die, but none has been able to kill me. Either they have not wanted to, once hearing my story, or their attempts have been in vain. The reforms that they have proposed have all sounded hollow to me–not because their plans seemed arrogant and dominating, even when they were seeking the good. I have been unable to see any reform which offers more than we had when I was King: love, justice, mutuality, and a spirit of individual development. I do not assert it, I just fail to see anything better…Well, now, do what you will with me."

I was dumbfounded by this story. Rather than wanting to kill this man, I loved him and wanted to serve him. Perhaps I was in the hands of the Devil, but somehow I preferred this man to anything of God that I had seen up until then.

I began to have strange, disquieting thoughts. Perhaps the Angel of God was the Devil and was leading us all to believe that this wise and kind King was causing the destruction that the Angel himself was causing. But could the Angel do this without the permission of God Himself? No! The next thought was too horrifying for me to consider...

I King looked at me in a strange, lovingly wise, but sad, way. "I know what you are thinking," he continued. "Many other Knights have thought of it before. You are thinking that God, Himself, is the Devil!" I shuddered as he said it, and expected at any moment to be struck dead. "Those who have come to it," he continued, "have either killed themselves, run from me in horror or agony, or quickly returned to their lives, pretending that they have not thought it.

"I do not know the answer myself. But I, too, have concluded that God cannot bear to look at his own darkness and destructiveness. He finds it easier to see it in Man, his loftiest creation on earth."

After thus hearing the King, I sat down, my body becoming a limp, muscleless mass. I had never been a very religious person, but I was sensible enough to know that Man was not the author of creation and that whatever God was, His ways were inexplicable to man and not to be deeply reflected upon. Before the Angel had appeared to me, I had not given it much serious thought. But now, I was forced to confront the issue more deeply. I could not challenge the reality of what I had experienced with the Angel, nor could I disavow what I was experiencing with this most human, and yet divine, King. What was I to do? What was I to follow?

The King sat in silence. He had said his say, and I was not inclined to disturb him. I was certainly not going to kill him, but what was I going to do about the Angel? Indeed, how was I to get back at all? I concluded that I had to go back and face the Angel with what I had experienced. Better to be killed for my failure to do the Angel's will than to outrage this excellent creature. And how was I to get back? The way I came, I supposed: to follow and trust in the horse.

I embraced the King, softly bade him peace and goodbye, took a deep breath from the air in the shell, clasped my horse's neck, and let go of my own will. Again, in the water. Again, the stretched lungs until I fainted.

Some time later, I found myself on land. Not at the point of entrance into the water, but at the place in the forest where I had seen the Angel, many days before. Had I dreamed all this? If so, it was as real as anything that had happened in my life until that time. I was uncertain if the Angel would appear again, but I was prepared to face him.

I sat down and waited. I looked at my horse and found him calm and most ordinary as if he had not, indeed, led me into and out of the depths of the Sea. What was the divine guidance which took him out of himself? What was the meaning of this paradox? I was sent by an Angel to kill a benevolent being, instead learned something profound from him, and was now alive and ready to confront the Angel who sent me on such a horrible mission!

Once more I waited seven long days and seven long nights. This time, however, I looked after the thirst and hunger of my horse and myself. I ate the fruit of the trees, drank the water of the stream, killed and hungrily devoured a deer that mischanced to come near my camp. On the evening of the seventh day, the Angel appeared again. Now he emerged just above the trees, radiant and in a white robe. His beard was white and he continued to look firm, but not as stern as the first time and much more benevolent than the second. This, too, startled me. Where was the evil? Where was the pain? The Angel spoke:

"My son, you have done as you were told. That was not a failure on your part, but a necessary experience which you had to undergo. The King has spoken truly."

But how can that be, O Angel of God? If the King has spoken truly, then you have lied. And how can the King be right, that God is not aware of his own destructiveness, if you are aware of it?"

"I have not lied, O Knight! Whom you saw at the bottom of the Sea was God, Himself! It is *He* who has forgotten his Godliness. It is *He* who was so ashamed of His power that He cut Himself off from it. It was *He* who so longed after becoming totally human and the brother of His creatures, that He rejected His power. And now it rules as madness in Heaven. The King, our Father, spoke truly of God not knowing of His darkness, and He was speaking of Himself. And I am that link, that piece of Him who is connected with both. But I can only do His bidding. I cannot bring Him to His senses. Were I to do so, His power would kill me, were He to want it or not. It is given to you, O Man, to bring this union about. It is given to you, if you survive, to let each know where the other is."

I sat quietly for a long time. My poor head was almost broken with this paradox. For this is what it was. Nothing less than that God Himself was split up in pieces and somehow needed Man, His creation, to bring Himself together. And this Angel, this divine messenger who linked with Man, he understood, but was powerless. What could Man do, who was far less powerful than an Angel, to bring the pieces together? If an Angel could be destroyed by the power, what would happen to poor Man? He would be burnt to a crisp, or driven mad! But now I saw why there was such confusion in the world: God was split in pieces. Man had to help God pull Himself together somehow. The new task of Creation was to be, indeed, a joint venture: Man and God as brothers and sisters, just as the King of the Sea had wished. But He, poor fellow, hadn't reckoned with His power!

What was I to do? How could I aid in this task? And why was I chosen? The answer came clearly. All and each of us, Everyman, had a piece of the divine spark and this was part of the plan for Salvation that God had spoken of long ago and, it seems, had forgotten. I understood what was meant by the stories of the past, when God walked with Man in peace and friendship. There was still the snake, the Devil-Son of God, who was disrupting and splitting and dividing, and God could not unite with him. So man had to unite himself within himself and, not only that, he had to help God do the same. Perhaps, at the End of Days, as the Ancients said, God would again be One, and Man would be One, too!

And that was the end of my first adventure.

CHAPTER 4
THE OLD WOMAN

Many years passed after I had completed the adventure which I have just described. I meditated about if often, but told no one about it. I was sure that I would either be scoffed at as a fool or madman, for everyone would be sure that all their troubles were a consequence of the vicious King at the bottom of the Sea. And who knows, maybe in a sense they would be right. A god who does not know his own power and quietly retreats from the world, letting that power wreak havoc without love, and without even being conscious of it, is, indeed, vicious in his ignorance. Still, I loved him and cared for him, and wondered how I could best serve him. I wondered too–for I had failed to ask him this question–if any other Knights had come to him, learned from him, and not committed suicide or forgotten their experience. Perhaps, somewhere I had a brother in spirit who was also puzzling about what to do.

The experience, however, changed my life. The issue was so great that all other adventures seemed paltry. I settled down, soon met a lovely woman and, in the course of things, we married and had three fine children–two girls and a boy. I tended my lands and my duties, but knew that one day I would be called upon again to serve in the task of re-uniting God with Himself. I strove to know myself as best I could and to unite the fragments of myself. It was a hard and painful task, but it was rewarding in itself. In time, a certain small fame came to me and I was able to help others come to more self-understanding.

It came to pass in my thirties, however, that I lusted after women once more. I had been a ladies' man in my early twenties, you may recall, but this had subsided after my experience of the Angel and King of the Sea, and I was happily married to a woman of great virtue and love, as well as understanding. This lust proved to be a peculiar one. It was not, as when I was a youth, that I wished to sleep with all the women in the world, but rather it was selective; the lust seemed to seek out just those women of some spirit, just those who were sore troubled in their knowledge and belief, and were pining away, without knowing it, for that God who was also at my back. I was sore troubled in my conscience for all this, for I was concerned lest I violate my marriage or myself. I was able to turn much of the passion to good use in the service of self-knowledge, both for myself and others, but there was always the additional part, which demonically would not be denied nor transformed.

One day, I walked again in the forest where I had had my encounter with the Angel, musing about my wickedness. I came to the spot and looked at it. A few years before, my faithful horse of my youth had died, after spending a peaceful old age, and I had buried him at the place where he had transcended himself and become both more of himself and his greatest self. For I had concluded that it was not just Man who had to aid in the task of divine transformation, but animals and plants, too. For they, too, carried the divine spark, did they not?

I looked at the grave and the simple stone I had erected thereon. It said, "To a faithful friend, from a faithful friend." I wondered about my fidelity, indeed. Had I really been faithful to this creature? Fidelity seemed to be a very questionable virtue with me.

As I looked, a mist collected over the stone. It was as if a certain essence emerged out of the stone itself, a soul-substance that gathered above it. It grew larger and larger, and glowed in the late afternoon dusk. Gradually the mist formed itself into a horse and rider. To my joy and astonishment, I recognized the outlines of my old trusted friend, with the Angel firmly seated upon his back.

"Greetings, O Knight," the Angel said. "It has been long since we have seen each other. But time is an illusion and, in the task of redemption, time is but a mist through which one walks to come to a clearer light. The mist you now see is more clear and real than the light by which you came to it."

I joyously ran forward to embrace both the horse and the Angel, but was stopped in my tracks just several yards away. The Angel spoke again: "Know, O Knight, that horse and rider are one. It was I, long ago, who led you from both above and below."

The Angel paused. I reflected that what he said did, indeed, make sense. I had been led by a heavenly spirit and by an earth spirit and they had, brought me to my understanding in loyalty and safety.

"Yes, Angel," I said, "I now understand. My instinct has been my guide, through you, from above and from below, and I have trusted it–and you. But my instinct has also gotten me into terrible trouble, as you, who walk to and fro in heaven, on earth, and in the sea, must know."

"I know, O Knight," continued the Angel, "for it has been only through that pain and power that you have been able to experience in your bones what you only understood in your head. But now your tortures are coming to an end, and the next phase of your development is about to take place."

With that, the vision vanished. In its place, I saw a yellow flower growing at the base of the stone. I plucked it from the earth and held it tenderly in my hand. I sniffed its fragrance and was so overpowered by its scent that I fell to my knees.

As if intoxicated by the fragrance of that golden flower, I felt myself whirling through smoke and clouds. The next instant found me under the earth, but in a vast place which looked much like above the ground in a volcanic region. Instead of sky, however, there were only the hard walls and ceiling of earth. A suffused light pervaded the place, pale blue in color. As my eyes grew accustomed to the light, I made out the form of a person lying on sand, near a body of water. I walked over to it and saw, clearly, a hag of a woman. She was disheveled, had old and torn clothes, and a face that was marred by ugliness. A stench was about her which was hellish. From all that I saw, I was certain that she was a witch. But then I looked into her eyes. They were dark and abysmal. In them I saw incredible suffering and agony. It was as if there were a continual shriek of pain coming from this being, but her silence was total.

I waited for her to speak, or to recognize my presence. I knew that she was aware that I was there, but I felt paralyzed and unable to initiate any conversation. I waited for a long time, feeling alternately chilled and heated in her presence. She could not or would not speak. I was powerless. Hours, days, weeks passed, or so it seemed. I lost all sense of time. As I sat there, I began to feel a nameless agony. I was reminded of all the pains of my life, physical and mental, and it was as if all of them were continuing for an eternity, without relief. When I thought I might go mad with grief and pain, I found that I could endure still more. I accepted it, not knowing why, just because. I then began to hear a voice, faint at first, but growing louder. I soon recognized the voice as the Angel's and looked around me to see where it was coming from. To my surprise, I could not locate the voice outside myself, and realized that it was coming from within. Somewhere in that shrieking mass of agony within my being, the Angel was speaking to me.

"Know, O Man. You see before you the figure of the woman, scorned. She it is who was the right hand of God. She it is who, on that day, long ago, when her son was crucified, took on herself the pain of Hell. And that pain is to suffer what men and God have suffered through eternity. Every hurt, every agony is registered there. She neither lives nor dies. She cannot speak. Indeed, she will not, until men take on their own agonies, and the agony of God as well. Are you prepared to take on her agony?"

Without thought or reflection, I nodded my assent, and I was filled with compassion. The intensity of compassion and of agony were exactly the same. I remembered a story about a boy, locked up in prison, because he was a Jew. He was then hanged for stealing a loaf of bread. I imagined him dangling there and understood the pain that this poor woman must have felt.

I knew, however, that my capacity for the endurance of pain and compassion was terribly limited. I had trouble coping with my own, let alone taking on that of the Goddess. I knelt in reverence. This was new for me. I had always bowed before the Most High, but to kneel was foreign to me. Now it came naturally. I knelt for a long time.

Though my eyes were half closed, I became aware of a change in the light. The suffused blue was being penetrated by a golden color. I looked up and beheld the figure of the Woman, transformed. She was as bright as the ball of the Sun and cast off a radiance which my poor eyes were less able to contain than my body and soul could contain the suffering. All the same, I felt healed and warmed. I felt, too, that new knowledge had come to me, which was hard to put into words. My lips began to form words of gratitude and devotion, but no sound emerged. Instead, I felt the loving embrace of the Golden Woman and was as over come with ecstasy as I had been earlier by pain. The joy was less long-lasting, due, no doubt, to my lesser capacity for enduring ecstasy–and I lost consciousness.

When I recovered my senses, I found myself again at the place in the forest where my adventures began. There was the gravestone of my horse, and there, in my hand, was the golden flower I had plucked earlier. Now, I could endure its scent and I sat down to reflect upon my experience.

The witch. The Goddess. The Wife of God and the Mother of God were all One. What did this mean? It meant that agony and ecstasy were one, and that they were endured by both God and Man. Glory and degradation, compassion and coldness, grief, joy, love and sin–all these are more belonged to God and to man, and they come through the Goddess, the right hand of God. Man is asked to endure all the human clash of heaven and hell, and the divine clash as well.

But, I reflected further, here is the Goddess, speechless, rejected by man, but also by God, or has He only forgotten Her? I thought of the King of the Sea and realized that since He has banished Himself under the Sea, His Wife is banished under the earth. And they are apart. Again the humpty-dumpty of God!

My task remained the same; to recover all those scattered parts of myself and to help God do the same.

What had changed? I could feel more intensely. I could also endure the conflict of opposites without running away. Best of all, the Angel seemed to find a home inside me. Could I dare to hope that this Messenger of God would stay?

I quietly wended my way home.

CHAPTER 5
THE EYE OF GOD

Only a few months after my second adventure, I grew restless in my need to bring about a union of the divine figures whom I had encountered. I experienced my own dividedness as a curse, yet I was sore afraid to encounter the Living Power who, in Heaven, was somehow responsible for the suffering I had seen. I did not know if the Angel would continue to guide me or if I was ready to seek out the way to the Power.

Troubled by these thoughts, I went back to the palace in the forest where my adventures had begun. I knelt and prayed for a dream to guide me. Very soon, I fell asleep and dreamed that a great bright star, the brightest in the heavens, had fallen from the sky and landed near the top of a mountain. I was wordlessly instructed to find this mountain and this star. I awakened with a start, but knew that this needed to be done, no matter what the cost. I proceeded back to my home, told my wife of my dream and my task. She painfully and quietly accepted it, though I knew that she feared for me. All the same, I lovingly bade farewell to my family and friends and, with the simplest provisions, set out to find mountain and star.

Many days I walked. And weeks. The weeks stretched into months. I walked through pale cities and hot deserts. I walked in the light of the moon and the heat of the sun. East, I walked. Often I was weary and hungry. Sometimes people helped me and were generous with what they had. At other times, I was kicked like a cur, and laughed at as a wandering fool. But most often people tended to shrink from me, seemingly in fear. I asked a wise man I met why this was so. He said only that I had "fierce, fierce eyes, with a fire in them, and people were sore afraid." I accepted what he said and, when I looked into a stream, found it to be true. Were these the eyes of the Goddess peering through me, I wondered, or a militant spirit which seemed excessive? I did not know.

The months passed and I sometimes lost track of why I was wandering. Forty months I wandered, until one day, after many days without food and many hours without water, in my trackless desert, I fell down in despair. I cursed myself and my fate, but my mouth could not even form the words. Dryness, cracked lips, and a grunt from my belly were all that stayed in my consciousness. Water, I wanted, and nothing else. I looked around me and, in a distance loomed a mountain, far away. Instantly I knew that it was *the* mountain. Again, as I had when confronted with the agony of the Goddess, I summoned up new resources and dragged myself along. After a time, when I walked only from memory, I nearly fell into an oasis. I drank deeply from the water and fell into a deep, dreamless sleep from exhaustion.

I do not know how long I slept, but I awakened refreshed. I ate fruit of the trees, replenished my supply of water, and continued on toward the mountain. As I walked onward, I noticed that the mountain was almost perfectly triangular in shape, and indeed not high at all. It looked grand and overpowering because it was unique in this desert, and compared to the flatness of the desert, was monarch.

At last I reached the base of the mountain and looked up. The face of it was sheer granite, unrelieved by crevices, except near the top, where a large slit strangely presented itself. As I wondered if I should attempt to climb this unclimbable thing–and, if so, how–the slit widened and I was confronted with a huge Eye. I quivered and trembled, but did not flinch from the encounter with this Eye of God.

The Eye looked at me coldly and fiercely and I knew, in an instant, that here was the greater Fierceness, of which the glint in my eye was but a paltry spark.

"Why do you come, O man?" The Eye spoke; how, I do not know, but it was if thunder and lightening were all around me. The Voice was everywhere and nowhere.

Shaken and awed, I held my ground, and said, "Because you sent for me."

The grew even fiercer. A rumbling took place within the mountain, which made me realize that it was a volcano. There came a crackling of the Voice, saying, "I did not! I go to and fro as I wish; I need no one and send for no one and surely not a mere Man, who is the author of such stupidity and viciousness in a world I regret that I created. Man, the crown of my creation, is lower than dust to me, and I do not know why I have not already obliterated him with a holocaust.

I was silent. What could I say? Could I tell this demon-God that He was the author of the stupidity and viciousness–at least the worst of it–and that He had already delivered so many holocausts that man was despairing of when the next and final one was to occur! I was reminded of what the Angel had said, that if he were to bring the darkness of God to His senses, the result would be the destruction of the Angel, were God to want it or not. For a mere mortal to suggest it would be to ask to be burned to a cinder.

"Speak!" said the Voice.

I continued to be silent. Whatever I might do would be wrong. If I spoke, I would be destroyed, and if I failed to speak I would be destroyed. Why, then, did the Angel tell me that it was up to Man to confront God with Himself? The Angel's words were burned into my soul: It is given to you, if you survive, to let each know where the other is." I must risk it, I thought.

At that moment, I understood. The Angel, indeed, was an aspect of God Himself, and that God was ready to destroy Himself, or a part at least, but had not, as yet, utterly destroyed men. I had to trust that I would not be destroyed, or, even if I were, other men would take up the task. Surely other Knights had seen what I had seen, and other Brothers would be summoned to the task.

With that realization, I looked up at the Eye once again, for I had been with my own eyes downcast during my reflections.

To my astonishments, the Eye seemed softer and filled with an infinite sadness. The sadness was not like the agony of the Goddess, who felt within herself all the pain and suffering of all creatures, human and divine, everywhere and of all time. Hers was the suffering that had been inflicted. His, however, seemed to bear the marks of one who is racked with guilt for having caused pain and agony. There was no self-pity and no flinching. In His silence, I knew, without words, that god was indeed aware of all the suffering He had caused, and that with his One Eye, he saw all that happened. I knew that He was aware of the whole course of history, and of His creations, but the He knew all of the future–of this I had doubt. I began to feel respectful compassion for this knowledge and suffering and for the Being who bore it, yet I was puzzled. This did not agree with what I learned from the King of the Sea, nor from the Angel. I was now confronted with something unexpected. God was aware of His darkness. How could I reconcile what I had learned from these three emanations of God?

I gazed in wonder at the Eye of God, opening without embarrassment, and in tense anticipation. I felt that, despite His protest, He wanted me to know. I waited patiently, knowing that I would get an answer to my unspoken questions.

I did not have long to wait. The Voice began to speak, not in wrath and thunder, but in a tone of quiet despair, much as a loving and wise father would speak to a younger friend about his children. He said:

"Long ago, I dwelt in peace with my creations. Man was my favorite and I lavished my bounty upon him, while he lavished his love upon me. We dwelt in happiness and mutuality. We lived in a garden, with all manner of good things to eat and all the pleasures of love and companionship. I saw my creation and that it was good, but I reckoned without my Son."

Here I was gripped with a deep nausea. It was a sickness that I could not account for. Was I reacting to the anticipated horrors of the old story of the snake? Or was I reaching to a kind of sentimentality in God Himself! I knew that on the human level brutal men lavish sentimental love on animals and plants, while condoning unspeakable tortures to other men.

"Your sickness is my sickness," God continued. "For then I was, indeed, unaware of my own destructiveness. I was a foolish father, who allowed poor mortal man to be tempted. And yet, I wanted it–I wanted them tested. I wanted my sons and daughters to grow and become partners with Me in the work of creation. With all my omniscience I could not entirely grasp the future, since I, too, was developing. And so, I shut my Eye, and allowed my Son to tempt man with knowledge. Man had everything but consciousness of himself, and this is my Son gave to him. He is, indeed, cold and hard, and reaches into the depths of the earth and the height of the stars. He wants consciousness above all, and at any price. My Son is surely a part of me, and inherits My lust to know. But His coldness and hardness is also passionate and even I am in awe of Him.

"His lust to know is also My lust. I have everything but knowledge of Myself—or, did so, until My Son gave man a light which is destined to make mankind My partner. *In the very act of giving light to man, my Son also gave light to Me.* That was a miracle I had not anticipated, having no real knowledge of Myself. My wrath was boundless, or nearly so. I would have destroyed Man altogether, if I did not realize that I needed him and that without the help of the divine spark I had given him, as well as the divine spark that my Son had given him, I would, indeed, be alone and that the task of creation would simply end. I was tempted, indeed, to start afresh, and make a new breed of man, yet I knew that I had made man in my own image and this was the best possible partner for the work.

"It took me long to fully grasp what had happened, and what I had done. When I saw the wickedness of men, from beginning to end, I was frequently tempted to start afresh. For, you see, My Son tempts me, too, and my consciousness was fitful. I caused much devastation, but always kept the race of men alive.

"In time, more men came to see the nature of my Son, and to both loathe it and adore it. Only a few saw that it was also my own Nature. As I grew in consciousness in my encounters with men, I came to loathe my Son and Myself. He was my firstborn and

I needed Him most, but the price in suffering was too high. What you perceived as my wife was in every greater agony. It was as if man's self-understanding and my Self-understanding were continually increasing, but it was becoming unbearable to Me.

"I began to see my own injustice, and how I was failing to live by the commandments that I had given man. I decided that with all my suffering, I did not really know how man suffers and that I must undergo that. But I could not undergo that totally, since the totality of my love and of my power would surely destroy man, at the stage of his development at that time. I decided to embrace my humanity and walk among men again, as a loving King. And I did, although I was not fully visible to them. I joined with a mortal woman (as I had done in the past with many heroes, but this time more consciously and resolutely) for the sake of creating my second Son, who was both God and Man, and would repair, in loving-kindness, what my First Son had destroyed with power. And it came to be. But, again, I had reckoned without my Power. Cut off from it, as I was, it began to act autonomously, and had its own aims. Again destruction, and I was forced to experience the greatest of all sacrifices a father can make: the sacrifice of his son. And He, the embodiment of Love, was crucified. I tasted what it meant to be man.

"With that, and in time, the sacrifice was of no avail, and wickedness, pain, grief, agony held sway. My Power banished my Humanity under the Sea, where you saw him as King of the Sea, and my own agony and suffering was banished under the earth, where you saw her as the Goddess.

"I have come back to my Power. Now, my First Son is more in the world than ever. In truth, He now lives and finds his home in Everyman. Again, this was a miracle of His which I did not anticipate. Where I had my Loving Being in one man-God, He has found His Being in all men. That is how it should be. The task of co-redemption is in earnest, and I cannot do it alone. I must be united with my Son, and Man must be united with Him also. For Love has never been enough. There must be Light. And more Light. 'Let there be Light,' I said, and it is done. Now there must be Light and Love, and Man must help Me to find it. My Eye sees many such Knights as you, who long after it, as I do. Go now and tell my message."

When the Eye and Voice had ended, I was in peace. I knelt and prayed for our mutual salvation and did so with both little self-consciousness and full self-consciousness for what I was doing. Then I looked up. I was aware that mists were rolling in from the Sea, far away, and from the earth. Then I knew that the King of the Sea and the Goddess of the Earth were coming back to the Center. In a moment, the Mountain turned to Gold and radiated a fantastic Light in all directions. It was a great Golden Triangle, with the Loving and Powerful Eye of God in the Center.

I was not deluded that my work was through. I felt privileged to witness this sight and knew that I would long reflect upon what I had seen and heard. I had no sense of exaltation, knowing that I now had a face an absent member beyond that Trinity, which would make it a Quaternity. And I knew that I had nowhere else to seek it but in myself. I had seen God's Wisdom, His Vision, His Humanity, His Love, and His Agony, but it was I who had to face, not His Power, but the one that dwelt inside me. In that task, I was neither alone, nor inept. For it required Everyman to do the same.

CHAPTER 6
THE SNAKE

When I came back from my third adventure, I was a more silent man. I knew that the task of knowing myself was more important than ever, and that my own struggle with the Snake-Son within me was the most significant work that I could do. I felt, too, the need to communicate what I experienced to other men, but I lacked the words to do so. In time, the momentousness of my experience waned, as I, like everyone, was caught up in the daily round of life. It was not that I lost track of the problem, but that my own feeling of power to do anything about it dissolved.

One day, as I was strolling in the forest where all of my adventures had begun, I felt a creeping sensation on my back and the rush of air my ear. It was as if a worm had crawled up my back and into my ear. It was as if a worm had crawled up my back and into my ear. I then heard a whisper:

"Look out, O Man, and not just within! I am

there, and here, and everywhere! Come and find me!" I reached into my ear, half-expecting to find a worm, but I found nothing and had only an itch. I looked about in my perplexity, but saw nothing. Then, with another rush of air, I felt the wind in my other ear, and heard the words, "Come to the south!"

I knew, now, with whom I had to deal, and, in a trusting way, immediately set off towards the south. This mercurial Being, I knew, would not give me time to settle my affairs, but, if I wanted to pursue him, I had to follow at once.

I walked quickly, waiting for him to give me a sign. As I walked, the landscape changed fantastically. At one moment I would be walking in lush tropical jungles, the next would fin me in cold arctic snows. Deserts and mountains came and went in the space of only a few steps. Cities with great monuments and forests with wild animals and men would appear and vanish with a change only in my breathing. I had the strong feeling of reality with each appearance and would be shaken the next moment by the changes. My belly and my heart were gripped alternately by them, but I resolutely kept up my pace. Without warning, the wind would whistle up my back and into one ear or the other, and I would hear the words, "You see?" or a crackling laugh. I had to confess to myself that I saw, but I did not understand.

After a time the visions I was presented with changed. Now the places I saw came slower and with a much heavier cast. I saw vast armies marching, and cities destroyed by war. I saw mounds of corpses in stinking piles, and great prisons where haggard men were in despair. I saw babies lying dead. Now the word came with the wind in my ear in a slower, heavier, and sadly ironic way: "You see?" These two words seemed laden with meaning, but still I could not grasp it. Yes, I saw, but I did not see. I saw, indeed, but I did not understand. My steps were slower. My own quickness and eagerness were slowed by my failure to understand.

I dragged one foot after another now, not in fatigue, but in despair of grasping what, apparently, I was being asked to understand.

Finally, I stopped and fell to the ground. I was spread eagled on the ground, lips to the dust. I tasted the dust on my tongue. I looked ahead of me and saw a long snake, thick and strong. His skin was a handsome black, with large red markings. He raised his head a few inches from me and spoke:

"Now, O Man, you know what it is to be ground into the dust! You want to know and to understand, and you do not! Well, lick the dust, as have I, for thousands of years. And you ask me why? I will tell you. It is because you want to know and understand!"

I accepted the words of the Snake, but still wanted to know: "Are you the Author of all this?"

"To know, to know!" he replied. "Of course, I am the author of it, and so are you, and so is Everyman who ever walked the face of the earth!"

Yes, of course, I thought, men have created all these things, and much of it was created by God–or by the Snake. There was nothing new in all that. What was the point of it all?

"Exactly!" responded the snake to my unexpressed thoughts. "Knowledge is Power, and what is the point of it all!"

"Are you telling me that it all leads to destruction and that Knowledge is the evil?" I asked.

"Questions, questions, questions! More knowledge, more power! More power, more destruction!"

Now, I became perplexed and irritated. This damned Son was just like his Father! Anything I did was wrong. If I asked a question, I was searching for knowledge which would lead to destruction. If I did not ask a question, I would still be stupidly wondering if I should abandon understanding altogether and simply live like an animal, which was out of the question. It was in my nature to know in the first place, and besides, this Devil tempted me to come follow him!

Laughter. Vast, rolling laughter. At first it was ironic and even sneering. Then it turned wide and joyous.

His laughter made me smile, though I felt rather like a fool for doing so. My irritation subsided, however, and again I had the peculiar feeling of no longer facing the Evil One. It was getting hard, indeed, to find the real Author of Evil in the universe!

The Snake was now arched on his back, making a large S, and chuckling quietly to Himself: "Devil am I? Yes, indeed. Disquieting and irritating am I? No doubt... What can I tell you, O Man? How can I really help you on your way? Yes, I am known as Satan, the Hinderer, but only because I interfere with men's wilfullness, not because I am opposed to them. Indeed, were you to ask my Father, He would say that I care more about Man than I do about the Father, Himself! No matter, each to his own scapegoat!

"Yes, Knowledge leads to Power, and Power leads to Destruction. It is so. But, in my Father's hands, Creation was the Power, and , before I offered the fruit, with His unknowing assent, the Creation led to destruction. His weeping caused rain, as every child knows. His angers were volcanoes; his lusts became jungles in an instant and his depressions were vast deserts. His thoughts were stars, and his deepest reflections a galaxy. He could not help but Create, and in His new Creations, an older creation was destroyed. He did not know this–or rather, He could not accept it and pushed this knowledge off on me. He desperately needed to know Himself. He needed a mirror for his existence. His first act therefore was to split himself. The first deed of God was that he divided Himself into pieces. In the beginning, there was One, then there were Two, then there were Four–and more. But He hated His division, and said, 'I'll make myself a Man, for company and pleasure.' But I knew, because He had given it unto Me to know, that He had made Man as a partner–to know Himself and to help Himself put Himself back together. But, since He made Man in His own image, Man, too, was destined to be divided. Because God loved Man, and hated His own division, He could not bring Himself to make Man aware of his division. That onerous task he gave to Me, His First Son, His dearly beloved and hated part of Himself. And so I am cast out, after having done my duty. Like you, I know what it means to be rejected unjustly!

"For long, I was only pushed away, not cast out. I was the needed insinuator–the one who would, like you, ask painful questions. I would look into things, into men's hearts and even God's heart and I would see things. At last, my Father could no longer stand Himself, nor Me, and He came to earth again, to show His Love. And His Second Son, a God-man, set out to redeem you all. He did a fair job, if evaluation is permissible, except that he not only left Me out, but made Me the author of all the Evil in the universe!

And why? Because I knew that God needed redemption Himself! That is the one bit of knowledge that the Father could not accept!

"My Brother did well. In His way, He tried to tell you, too, 'Ye are Gods! he said. But few seemed to realize what He meant. So, He died, was sacrificed, and you know the rest."

At this point, the Snake stopped, and seemed to withdraw into Himself. I wanted Him to go on, but was fearful of getting into one of those paradoxical question-puttings again. All the same, I tried:

"But," I said, "Your Brother is said to have Ascended and that He would be born again."

The Snake smiled. "Do you believe it?" He asked.

"Well," I responded. "That is hard to say. I am a Jew, you know, though a Knight. But in my heart, I am also a Christian, and an ancient Greek, and some others as well."

The Snake laughed uproariously again, "Of course," He chortled. "I told you that I see into souls, and I see that you are divided! No matter, so are they all, especially those that think they are not!"

"Will He come again?" I persisted.

"Of course He will. It is so written."

Again, I paused. I needed to reflect upon what I had been told and, since the Snake seemed content to wait a little, I gave myself the time to think.

In actuality, many days went by before I could again speak to the Snake. Part of me was very much back in the world, in life, involved in the daily round and even intensely so. The other part of me remained there facing the S-shaped Snake in silent wonder. In this very act of living in both places, I had a deeper understanding of the Snake and of God's division: one knows and one does not know; one is there and one is not there. Now the division was less painful to me. It was, indeed, as the Angel once told me, that the need was "to know whether the other one is" both for god and man. The division was tolerable as long as one knew that there was a development, an end, a quest. What was more natural for a Knight than to be on a quest?

When I returned my full attention to the Snake, He smiled. I was aware of a golden crown on His head, and He softly repeated words that I had heard long ago and were now etched in my memory: "Summoned or not, God is always present."

After this time of silence, the Snake continued: "I have made you aware of only a part of My nature, which is 'to know.' As you are well aware, 'to know' is also a passion. It was written in the old books that 'to know' also means 'to unite with'–to passionately desire union. You experience Me in that way, too, as your passion to unite. Sex, you call Me, and a demon, and so I am, for I am satisfied with nothing less than total union. Restrain Me, you must! I know full well, for union without love is disastrous. Not only you know that, but many have know that. There are those that call Me Kundalini, for I crawl into the holes and crevices of the spine and to every center that I can find, to go up and up and down and down, until all that is to be known is known and all that is be united with is united. Do not fear Me, though you are right to fear Me–but only if you do not know me and value Me. Without Me, there is no life, no press, no pull. There are those, both East and West, who would deny Me, and overcome Me, and reject Me. They are right to try, though doomed to failure. They can kill Me, and experienced death themselves, but, as long as there is life, I am reborn. And after death, too, as my Father well knows.

"Passion I am, and passion I will be. Listen to Me and heed Me, and also do not heed Me. That is my message. If you understand you are blessed, if you do not you are damned."

I understood. One had to go with one's passions and restrain them. And one had to listen from moment to moment. The Angel's message was sound: "let each know where the other one is!" In the face of division, keep connected with the parts. And Evil? What was Evil? Evil was division, not knowing oneself, where the Other was. Power without love; Love without wisdom; Wisdom without passion; fundamentally, God without man and man without God. I understood. And I trusted.

I looked up again at the snake. He had changed. I now saw a hermaphroditic creature, male and female, united, but back to back. Each wore a crown. I nodded and knew that there was union, but that it was incomplete. I knew that I had much more to do, more to know, more to love, and more to live, before the total union was possible. I nodded and bowed.

My honest submission to this being seemed to cause a change in Him. The Snake transformed back into his original form and leaped high into the air. He went straight for the marvelous golden triangle where the Eye of God glowed. He wrapped himself about this triangle and penetrated into its core. An explosion of light. Now the triangle was golden as before, but surrounded by the circle of the Snake, biting its own tail. In the center of the triangle was the Eye of God, with a human King on one side and a human Queen on the other, facing, and united. A funny arithmetic: three plus two equals four.

It was enough. And I went back to my life.

CHAPTER 7
THE YOUNG GIRL

After my fourth adventure, I thought that I understood and could now live my life in a more meaningful and creative way–but I was mistaken. It was true that I understood much more and I experienced a greater sense of inner union, as well as a sense of greater union in the divine, but still…Doubt and dissatisfaction again gnawed at me. Was this simply the greed of the old Adam in me, I wondered, or was the Snake sending me a message? After some time of letting the problem brew, I once again returned to my sacred place in the forest where all my adventures began.

I walked leisurely through the trees, enjoying their fine scent. I listened to the crackling of leaves underfoot and felt the chill of autumn. The reds, browns, and golden hues of the leaves played with the greens stunningly. As I looked at this great display of nature, I realized that what I had not seen in my encounters with God, had been this: Beauty, Art, Joy, Play. Yes, play. Was this universe really so totally serious and desperate all of the time? Or was it my own serious nature that simply filtered out of all experiences just those that were hard and difficult and concerned with the dark and puzzling side of life?

Harkening back to my youth, before the Angel appeared, I recalled how I had responded to Music, to Art, to games with my friends. Yes, there had been Joy, but the Angel's stern "No" put an end to that. Was Play, then, only in Man's province? Were Art and Beauty Man's creation alone? As I looked at this forest, I realized that God must love beauty, too, or He would not have made it so dazzling since no eye but His had previously gazed on it.

Relieved, I sat down by the side of a stream to refresh myself. I lazily let my hand dip into the cold water and both welcomed and resisted the gentle flow as it coursed by me. I laughed at myself. Even when I wanted to be lazily playful, I had to test myself! I was God's fool, indeed!

It was then that I hear the singing. How can I describe it and not simply echo what poets have said? Yes, that is it! It was, of course, the singing that poets have heard and have attempted to translate into words and into music. I am neither poet nor musician, but I will try to tell you, in the simple language I have used until now, just what it was that came across my path.

I followed in the direction of the singing and came into a clearing. There, not more than twenty paces from me, but totally oblivious of me, was a girl of perhaps sixteen, sitting by the stream, and combing her long dark hair. She was pretty, yes, but not at all preoccupied with it. She was pretty in the way that the trees are pretty.

Again I laughed at myself. My own nature and even God's will, both for Himself and for me, was that I become as conscious of myself and of Him as possible. The chief sin was unconsciousness. Here, before my eyes, was a creature that seemed totally unaware and yet was the most beautiful being that I had ever seen! I laughed again and said to God: "Well, Sir, what do you make of that!"

Since no response from God was forthcoming, I settled back to listen to the singing. She sang songs that were gay and songs that were sad, and she sang them in language after language. I understood some of these languages, and I even remembered hearing some of the songs before. Others were utterly foreign to me, and in modes and styles that I tried to follow, but couldn't because they were unexpected in their changings. There were subtleties beyond my grasp. I wondered, how could this girl–clearly young, protected, naive, unknowing–sing in all these tongues with such authority? Her accent and understanding were perfect in those languages with which I had some acquaintance and I had to assume that this was also true for the many others. She could hardly have learned all these languages in her brief span of life. Was she, then, simply a great parrot, or–I caught my breath in disbelief–a Goddess? And why, I asked myself, was I so disbelieving? Why could she not be a Goddess? Was I, indeed, so prejudiced as to think that God could not manifest Himself as a Herself, and a sixteen year old, as well? I recalled my experience of the Goddess of Suffering, and chided myself on my limited patriarchal viewpoint. With that, I decided to keep myself open to what would happen.

I listened to the singing for a long time, keeping my eyes closed in order not to be distracted by anything else. Softly, she sang, and then loudly. Sometimes her voice was romantic or wistful, sometimes she sang passionately of love, of rage, of scorn. There even were martial songs which stir the blood against one's will, and my own blood responded. Then the songs stopped.

I looked up to see what had happened, why they had stopped, and was startled to see the girl bending over me, intently.

"Who are you? she demanded, and "And what are you doing here?'

"I am just an ordinary Knight," I replied, "And I often walk in this forest. I heard your singing and was enchanted by it." I said this in as forthright a manner as I could, but I was feeling guilty at the invasion of her privacy, so I added, more meekly, "I am sorry to have intruded."

She seemed perplexed by this, but did not speak another word. Instead, she moved away a few steps, darted among the trees and brought back with her a woman who seemed to be in her late thirties, obviously her mother.

The mother was as stunning, in her way, as the daughter was in another. The elder woman was also dark, but full-bodied, more sensual, and experienced. As a pair, they were a marvel, and since I was still lying down, I was both awed and slightly frightened.

They looked at me sternly. I had the amusing thought that they must, indeed, be Goddesses, because every time I met another manifestation of God it was a stern one! With that, I laughed, got to my feet, and said, in my most charming, knightly way (gathering memories from my youth, when I was, indeed, as I have said, something of a ladies' man), "Ladies, I beg your pardon if I have disturbed you, but I can only plead that I have been utterly enchanted with your singing, Miss, and with your beauty, Madam!" I then flourished my hat and bowed deeply.

To my chagrin, the ladies were not, apparently, at all enchanted with me, and simply turned on their heels and walked off.

I was bemused. What did I do wrong? I was a gentleman, I thought, and this manner had its appeal with other such ladies. But was I really a gentleman? Inside? Obviously not, and I knew it. Perhaps these ladies knew it, too. I was impressed. I should have added, "At your service!" Ah, that was it! If they were, indeed, Goddesses, they would expect that from me, of course. I had dedicated myself to the service of God, but I had failed to include my dedication to the Goddess!

With that realization, I ran after them, this time genuinely ready to ask their pardon–not for intruding, but for not being ready to serve them. I ran only a few steps and there they were in front of me, with broad smiles and open arms. Again, I was startled. Could they read my thoughts so quickly and change so radically in response to them? They were Goddesses, indeed!

"We are, O Knight," began the elder, in response to my unspoken question. "We have long wondered when you would finally realize it and seen Us out."

"I have not sought You out, good Ladies," I replied, "because I have been almost totally engrossed in the religion of the Fathers and of the Sons. I have been preoccupied with the problem of evil, and of consciousness, and, above all, the problem of meaning. But, I think, I have met you in another form, have I not? There, under the earth, in that great cavern?'

"No," the elder woman replied. "She whom you met was my Mother and indeed, only in one form. One day, please God, you will meet her in another, which will not be so enlightening for you."

I chose, at that moment, to hold my tongue and not ask my questions. It was enough that I was now meeting with a human sort of Goddess. I was in no hurry to meet a fate that I was not at all sure I was ready for. I waited for the Goddess to go on.

"You have met Me, dear Knight" (I was startled and pleased at this hint of endearment) "at other times, and perhaps you did not know it. You have met me whenever you have felt attracted to a woman, felt yourself drawn to her as if to a beloved, or a long forgotten sister. For I am, indeed, that soul-sister whom you have encountered often. Do not conclude that I exist only in your imagination, or that you mistakenly experience me as coming from outside of you. No, that is not true. A man would like only too much to believe that, since it is so convenient. It would give him a chance to escape from life, but it is not true. Yes, indeed, I do make my home inside you, should you only desire it or acknowledge it, but I also live in them, in all those women to whom you are attracted, and–I must add–repelled.

"For, you see, my realm is life. My realm is love and hate and connections. My realm is a web, an invisible church of entanglements. The magnetism of attractions and repulsions, of involvements and estrangements, not only between men and women, but among young and old, and of these among themselves. People experience Me, and are shaken. They are shaken out of their masculine will and whisper of reincarnation, of soul-mates, of brothers, of sisters. In short, I am She who brings about union and it's opposite. You ask for meaning. Do you not know that there is no meaning with Me!"

Here, the Goddess grew angry, and I had to acknowledge that She was right. I had given lip-service to Her, in my acceptance that there was no meaning without experience, but I was secretly, as She had hinted, gathering my experiences of life in order to be free of it. I was like a Hindu, I suppose, engaged in life and its illusion, only to be free of it. I took life as a sponge would take water, only to drain it into some private little vessel of aloneness. I bowed to her and sighed quietly.

The Goddess softened. She looked at me with compassion. "I know that is so," She continued. "In reality, I do not blame you for it. For you must, as a man, be a man, and free yourself of illusion and entanglements. But you only have to acknowledge Me, to expect Me, to understand Me, for I am not opposed to your blessed consciousness, I am only opposed to its one-sidedness. That is My nature, to bring together. The Angel once told you that the task is 'to let each know whether the other is.' That is true. But I am the one who brings the each to the other! It is not just you that has overlooked me, and forgotten me. God knows, you are better than most men in this regard! It is the Father…"

Here the Goddess grew rueful and seemed to vanish inside Herself, just as She did when She grew angry with me. I felt that Her dialogue with me was also a dialogue with Another, which I dared not suggest to Her. She knew it anyway, I suppose.

She was silent a long time. I looked at Her, in Her silence, and felt echoes of deep thoughts and questionings that were going on in a language that I could not fathom at all. It was a mystery of a feminine thinking–a kind of consciousness which would, perhaps, always remain a mystery to me. I could only wait, in respectful communion with Her, knowing that I was not in real communion, but that I was just with my own images and not where She was. I smiled wryly to myself, feeling a barbed criticism toward Her. She was the one who opted for not only "letting each know where the other is" but also to bring about union, and now her thoughts were elsewhere, quite apart from me!

"You are right, O Knight," the Goddess continued. "I am, indeed, guilty of what I complain about, and that is exactly where I was at that moment, speaking with the Father."

Her face changed again, from an intense and fathomless searching to a smiling warmth. Her Daughter, now, was playing with pebbles and leaves and humming to Herself. There was an atmosphere of peace, even of play, but there was also something uncanny going on.

The Goddess' face was warm, but strained. She had not, indeed, totally returned to me. I did not mind that, but I sensed a growing tension in the air. It was quiet, but the air was heavy, as if before a storm. I instinctively reached for my sword and glanced about me looking for the danger. The forest, too, was silent. No birds were singing, no wind was blowing. All the myriad forest sounds were stilled. I peered at the Goddess to see if She were aware of this strange silence. She only watched Her happy Daughter, playing innocently with the pebbles. There was an infinite sadness in the eyes of the Goddess, which reminded me of Her Mother.

I said nothing, but kept my hands on my sword. When the stillness was at its height, when I thought my nerves would crack with the tension, when I thought I could stand it no more, I heard an unearthly sound.

It was a laugh, but not a laugh, a cackle; and not a cackle, but a great, horrendous, female, blood-curdling sound which seemed to wreck the Universe or, at least, all the order in it. I shivered and trembled and drew my sword like a demon, ready to fight the Unknown.

There came, from out of the forest, a horde of faces and bodies, some whole and some in parts. There came men and women of every race–black, brown, white, red, yellow. There came creatures who were part man and part animal, all the kinds that I had ever seen in bestiaries and many more besides. There came plants with feet. And they came in a wild dancing, a mindless play and lust that threatened to tear us apart.

I looked to the Goddess, to see if She could stop this invasion. She observed the creatures, was sad but impassive. I glanced at the Daughter, now on Her feet in utter terror.

I knew that I had to fight. I realized that I would lose, and probably die, but I had to devote myself for the Goddesses. I leaped in front of them and fought like a tiger. I fought harder than I ever had in my life, and I was always known as something of a battler. I fought and I slew. Bodies were piled upon bodies as I slew; limbs and arms and blood and gore, until I was covered with it in a great pile all around me. I suffocated from the scene, the stench, and from the agony of my own wounds. I lost consciousness.

When I awakened, I was once again in the great cavern underneath the earth, where I had encountered the Great Mother Goddess. But the landscape was different. Instead of the starkness and the blue light, all was now in green and red and yellow. There was lush vegetation with forms and shapes which were fantastic to me. I was conscious of my environment before I was aware of myself. First, I felt pain and restraint. I was tied to a tree. To my left was the Goddess, also tied to a tree, and to Her left, the Daughter, in the same condition.

The creatures, human and otherwise, were all around us, demonically laughing and dancing. Now, they descended upon up again, incubi and succubi. They crawled into every orifice of my body and sucked all my juices–saliva, urine, semen, sweat, blood. At first I was outraged, but I reflected: I have been raped in the spirit so many times, why should I be so outraged by a rape of the flesh?

When my head was free for a moment, I turned to look at the Goddess and the Daughter. The Goddess was unmoved. She stood in stoic and grand calm before this assault. Without having seen it, I knew that She, too, had fought like a tigress, but was holding Herself and Her humanity high before this assault. But then I saw the Daughter. Her face was tortured, and the agony in Her eyes was as great as that of the Great Mother Goddess whom I had seen long ago.

Then I heard someone crying.

I turned to see who it was that was crying. It was not the Goddess; it was not the Daughter; it was myself. I wept. I sobbed. The tears ran in a way that they had not since childhood. Nay, not even in childhood had I wept so. I wept for myself. I wept for what it was to be a man, to be human, and even to be a creature.

The tears, too, were consumed by the demons, and my pride went. Not that I was humiliated–I was somehow beyond that. Rather, I felt that these demons and people were just like myself; they killed and raped and devoured and were, in turn, killed and raped and devoured. So be it.

Suddenly–with the same abruptness with which I had heard the great cackle–all was silent. The cavern was suffused with green light of every imaginable shade. There was a Presence. I knew that I was about to bear witness to the Great Mother, and in a very different way than I had seen Her before, just as Her Daughter had warned.

In the midst of the green light, there appeared a great Mouth with lips as red as the light was green. The lips parted and spoke, though the words came from outside Her and everywhere at once. Her words, unlike the crisp clarity of the Father, echoed and reverberated. With each word, there was born some creature, pouring out of her mouth. She spoke:

"For three thousand years, O Man, I have been rejected! For three thousand years! But you have known Me in a million guises: as lust, as hunger, as meat and bread, and earth, and wine. You have known Me, and lusted after Me, and rejected Me. The more you reject Me, the more I am as a demon to you. Nature is My realm, and it is as it is: in pleasure and in pain, in creation and destruction. You, O man, would despoil it and ravish it and devour it and consume it. For love, or for desire? Oh, no! For power, for consciousness, and for such other soarings of the Spirit as your malicious little minds can devise. But My day is coming! O Man! Now you see Me, in your wars, and your impotencies, and your hungers. Now you see Me. Until you accept Me, I shall crawl into every opening and devour every bit of you. Sovereignty!"

I was silent. What could I say? It was true that we men had exploited nature, harmed her, used for our own ends. It was true that we men had so treated women–and the Goddess. It was true that we had rejected Her, or at least many of us had. But I had the feeling that she was speaking not only to me, but to Another. Her bitterness and resentment should be against the Father, really, since we poor mortal men were abysmally ignorant, stupid and impotent. Dare I tell Her that? Dare I tell her that I saw Her traces, indeed, in both the Father and in Her Snake-Son?

I said nothing. Words were not necessary. She knew, of course, "where the other one was." The lips vanished and there was silence.

I felt my bonds loosen and fall away. The Goddess, the Daughter, and I were now free and among men and the creatures. The men and the creatures had changed. Their forms were the same, but the demonism had disappeared. We wandered freely among them, and there was a sense of belonging all together.

I knew, though She had not said it, that the Great Mother was really against me because of my secret pride, my chosenness, my individuality. The Great Father could not tolerate His own unconsciousness (or mine), and the Great Mother could not tolerate my uniqueness. Had I really understood? Was She, indeed, opposed to uniqueness? No, she was opposed to that uniqueness, that chosenness, which set a man apart from other men, in pride and in isolation. We are all chosen, after all, with a divine spark.

With that realization, my heart lightened and I could get a glimpse of that day "when all mankind will be as brothers", and we mustn't forget the animals, and the plants, and the angels, and the demons. When the All will be as One.

The next moment found me in my sacred place in the forest. All was quiet and serene. Ahead of me, just above the trees, I again saw the Golden Triangle, shimmering. At its apex was the Eye of God, the Father. At the left corner stood the King of the Sea, god the Brother, all in blue. In the right corner coiled the Snake, God the Son, black and red.

Then, out of the depths of the earth, there appeared another triangle, dark and green with an intensity as great as the Golden Triangle. But this triangle was reversed. At its nadir was the Mouth of the Great Mother, as red as rubies or pomegranates; God the Mother. At the left corner stood the Goddess, radiant in red; God the sister. At the right corner knelt God the Daughter, in a lovely yellow.

Together, the triangles made a Star of David. I was astonished. The symbol that had been spat upon, rejected, was there in all glory and in a new light. I thought: It is right. From this union will come Another. The Messiah. The seed of King David. And this Son will be the awaited First Coming of the Jews, the Second Coming of the Christians, and the Reborn Son of the Greeks. So be it.

I bowed in reverence, and was suddenly transported into the Center of the Star. There was I, a king without a crown, just like all humanity. We all belonged there. I had hope. On that day, when He comes, the Star will come to Earth, and we will all be as One.

CHAPTER 8
THE TREE OF LIFE

My fifth adventure seemed to satisfy most of my doubts and questions, and gave me a new sense of purposed and well-being. I returned to my family and friends, eager to share with them what I had experienced. Most of them were moved by my story and understood very well what they were all about. New doubts assailed me, however. Was their reaction only because they knew me and loved me, or was what I had experienced of a more general nature? In short, would people who did not know me and care for me also find meaning and value in what I had discovered?

This question pressed at me and would not let me rest. Once again I was harassed from within to go on a quest, but this time the need was to connect with my fellow man.

Now I wandered in places I had never seen before. I met Jews and Christians, Muslim Arabs and Buddhists from Japan. I met Africans who had very different stories–all about animals–which moved me greatly. I met Hindus and Atheists. I would try to tell my story and got many kinds of response. Some would nod their heads and say, "Yes, that is the way it is." Others would say, "What a nice story!" These reactions pleased me. There were other responses, however, which puzzled me. They said such things as: "No, you have got it all wrong! That is not the way it is at all!"; "Yes, you have a partial truth, but the real truth is this (and then they would tell me their stories)"; "What mad fantasies! Don't you know that God is just a creation of men's imaginations?"; "Are you insane?"; "What presumption!"; "Don't bother me with such silliness!"; God is dead, why try to revive him?"; and, finally, "Heresy!"

I returned to my home bemused. What was I to make of all that? Naturally, I went to my sacred place in the forest in order to sort out what I had experienced. I sat down and rubbed my chin. My story spoke to some and not to others–that was clear. How could that be? I was sure that God had spoken to me. Could some of these people be right and others wrong? Or was it, indeed "only a fantasy"? In any case, everyone seemed to be an authority.

In my puzzlement, I chanced to look up. There, before my eyes, was a gigantic tree. The trunk was huge and stretched higher into the heavens than my eye could reach. One could guess that its' roots reached down into the earth and spread through it in an equally vast way. I was stunned. I had never seen this tree before. Had it grown suddenly overnight!

I looked at the strange fruit of this tree. Instead of oranges and lemons and pears, there were signs and symbols. There were stars and crosses of every shape and description. There were circles, and squares, and crescents, and all manner of geometric shapes. There were phalli and breasts and other parts of the body. There were even trees and plants. Many of the symbols were rich and lush with many colors; others were old and dying. And buds, buds in great profusion.

As I looked on in wonder and bewilderment, I suddenly glimpsed my own Star of David, at the end of one branch. There it was, lovely and shining! The figures therein smiled out at me and waved. I waved back and felt foolish.

A moment later, there appeared, no longer in a mist but in a concrete way, the Angel of God, mounted on my horse. He carried a flaming sword, but He, too, smiled at me and waved. The Angel spoke:

"What you see before you is the Tree of Life. It was always there, but you did not know it. All the fruit thereon grows and thrives and dies. New ones take their place. The sap of the tree, the blood of God, courses through them, and they enrich each other. The fruits nourish mankind and help him live. When his particular fruit dies, he dies. Until he finds another one, his soul is dry. So it has always been, and so it will always be.

"The many fruits of the tree are immortal and man is immortal. So are you immortal, Sir Knight. Here have I stayed with my flaming sword since that first day, when the first man and woman did eat of that other tree. God, the Father, put me here, and said:

'Behold the man is become as one of us, to know good and evil; and now, lest he put forth his hand, and take also of the tree of life, and eat and live forever…'

"But man was already immortal, though God did not want him to know it until he was ready. And man was not ready to know until he was ready to accept and understand what was meant when God said, 'man is become as one of us'. Now you understand, and the flaming sword no longer bars the way."

The Angel finished speaking and vanished into the tree. I fell on my face with joy and gratitude and, for the first time in my life, sang the praise of God.

After a time, I stood up again and looked at the tree. I knew that my sacred place in the forest was nothing else than the Garden of Eden, though I never knew it. I held out my hands, and the luminous Star of David came off the tree right into my palms. I did not eat, because I had not need to eat, but I put it next to my heart.

In duet, I heard the voice of the Angel and the Goddess saying, "Let each know where the other is."

So, here is my story, O Brother. Here is where I am. Where are you?

REFERENCES
1. Jung, C.G. *Psychological Types*. Routledge and Kegan Paul, London, 1923. Also Collected Works, Vol. 6.
2. Jung, C.G. *The Transcendant Function,* orig. 1916, published in Collected Works, Vol. 8.
3. Jung, C.G. *Memories, Dream, Reflections*. Pantheon Books, New York, 1961.
4. Jung, C.G. *Letters*. Vol. 1: 1906-1950. Princeton University Press, 1973.
5. Jung, C.G. *VII Sermones ad Mortuos*. Stuart and Watkins, London, 1961, Orig. 1925.
6. Weaver, Rix. *The Old Wise Woman, a Study of Active Imagination*. G.P. Putnam's Sons, New York 1973.